Cedric Ceballos

by Mark Stewart

ACKNOWLEDGMENTS
The editors wish to thank Cedric Ceballos for his cooperation in preparing this book.
Thanks also to Integrated Sports International for their assistance.

PHOTO CREDITS
All photos courtesy AP/Wide World Photos, Inc. except the following:

Vince Manniello/Sports Chrome – Cover, 4 bottom right, 5 center right, 6, 45, 47 bottom right
Cal State Fullerton – 13, 14, 20 top left
Los Angeles Lakers – 43
Mark Stewart – 48

STAFF
Project Coordinator: John Sammis, Cronopio Publishing
Series Design Concept: The Sloan Group
Design and Electronic Page Makeup: Jaffe Enterprises, and
            Digital Communications Services, Inc.

LIBRARY OF CONGRESS CATALOGING-IN-PUBLICATION DATA
Stewart, Mark..
    Cedric Ceballos / by Mark Stewart.
      p. cm. – (Grolier all-pro biographies)
    Includes index.
    Summary: A biography covering the personal life and basketball career of the
All-Star forward with the Phoenix Suns and the Los Angeles Lakers.
      ISBN 0-516-20164-6 (lib. binding) – 0-516-26013-8 (pbk.)
      1. Ceballos, Cedric–Juvenile literature. 2. Basketball players–United States–Biography–
Juvenile literature. [1. Ceballos, Cedric. 2. Basketball players. 3. Afro-Americans–Biography.]
I. Title. II. Series.
GV884.C43S84 1996
796.323'092–dc20
    (B)   96-13116
                                                                                      CIP
                                                                                       AC

Grolier **ALL-PRO** Biographies™

Cedric Ceballos

by
Mark Stewart

CHILDREN'S PRESS®
A Division of Grolier Publishing
New York • London • Hong Kong • Sydney
Danbury, Connecticut

Contents

Who

Am I?

When I was a kid, I lived very close to where my favorite team, the Los Angeles Lakers, played basketball. I never actually went to a game. I couldn't afford to. Now I play for the Lakers. It just goes to show that sometimes even the craziest dreams really do come true. My name is Cedric Ceballos, and this is my story . . . "

"Sometimes even the craziest dreams really do come true."

Growing Up

When Cedric Ceballos was four years old, his grandmother took him down to the local elementary school and enrolled him in the first grade. The other kids in his class were a year or two older, but Cedric had no trouble keeping up. The only thing he found difficult was reading. He knew his alphabet as well as any of his classmates, but the words he saw in books did not always make sense. Cedric did not want to fall behind, so he asked his teachers for help.

It turned out that Cedric had a mild case of dyslexia, a learning disorder that affects a person's ability to read words on a page. Cedric recalls, "I knew that the letters on the page made a word, but sometimes I had to look for a long time before that word popped into my head. I knew I wasn't stupid. I just saw things differently than other kids. The toughest thing about having dyslexia was reading aloud in class. It could be very embarrassing. Eventually, I got used to it and learned to adjust."

Cedric was a good student. He liked most of his subjects, especially math. Cedric felt much more comfortable with numbers than he did with words. Still, he knew how important it was to learn how to read. As Cedric worked harder and harder and eventually overcame his dyslexia, he proved that no obstacle is too big to defeat. "You can't get through everyday life without knowing how to read," says Cedric. "It is very important. Words are part of the world!"

Cedric grew up like lots of kids in Los Angeles, California. He went to school, played with his friends, and tried to avoid confrontations with older kids, many of whom were in gangs. Most of all, Cedric dreamed about one day becoming a member of the Los Angeles Lakers, who played just a few miles away from his home. He and his friends liked to go to the nearby basketball courts and pretend that they were the team's stars: Kareem Abdul-Jabbar, Jamaal Wilkes, and Norm Nixon. In 1979,

Cedric fulfilled a boyhood dream when he ended up playing for the Los Angeles Lakers.

Magic
Johnson

the Lakers drafted Magic Johnson. Soon everyone wanted to play exactly like Magic—everyone, that is, except Cedric. Cedric did not dribble well and he was not a great shooter. In fact, whenever he got the ball, his teammates would yell at him to pass it right away. No one ever yelled that way at Magic. Cedric decided that he would not make a very good point guard, so he began to hang around the basket waiting for other players to miss their shots. When the ball clanked off the rim, he would grab the rebound and put it right back up from close range. Little did he know that this playing style would take him all the way to the NBA one day . . . where he would play alongside Magic himself!

Kareem Abdul-Jabbar

edric remembers, "I wasn't a superstar at the parks. In order to get the ball, I had to get the garbage from offensive rebounds or a loose ball. Then everybody would yell so fast to pass it to them, I had to shoot it quickly—if I wanted to score, that's how I had to do it."

When Cedric turned 15 years old, he decided he was good enough to try out for the Dominguez High School varsity basketball team. He impressed the coach with his unselfish play and his ability to come up with loose balls. Cedric made the team but played only a few minutes a game in his junior year. After gaining a little weight and a lot of experience, he played a lot more the following season. Cedric did not start until his final game, although he did contribute about 12 points a game. It was enough to help the team, but not nearly enough to earn him a college scholarship.

Cedric graduated from high school at the age of 16. He wanted to continue his education and keep playing basketball, so he joined several spring leagues in the Los Angeles area. Cedric hoped to impress recruiters and earn a scholarship. When Ventura Junior College coach Phil Mathews invited him to play for his team, Cedric accepted. He would be one of the youngest students on campus, and by far the youngest player on the team.

College

When Cedric Ceballos showed up for the first day of practice at Ventura Junior College, no one suspected that the tall, skinny 17-year-old would quickly become the school's star. But soon everyone saw that Cedric possessed raw talent. When his teammates had the ball, he was always moving, looking for an opening, trying to establish position under the basket. He did not have slick moves or a great shot, but whenever he got the ball he found a way to put it in the basket. Cedric would go through an entire game without making a single spectacular play, yet he was usually the game's high scorer. In his second season with Ventura, he averaged more than 28 points a game—more than any other junior college player in California. Scholarship offers from big-time schools began rolling in.

Again, Cedric decided to stay close to home. He accepted a scholarship to play his final two college seasons for California State University at Fullerton. The school offered a competitive

Years

basketball program and good courses in communications, which is what Cedric wanted to study. Fullerton also had a special program for students with learning disabilities, so Cedric could learn more about dyslexia, and how he could live with it.

Cedric attended California State University in Fullerton.

At Fullerton, Cedric blossomed into a premiere small forward. He was the team's high scorer in most of its games, and he won the Big West Conference scoring title. Cedric's senior year was even better. He led the conference in scoring again, and finished among the top ten rebounders in the country. He also was named All-Big West for the second year in a row.

idway through Cedric's final season at Fullerton, his teammates began noticing pro scouts in the stands. They knew who they were there to see: Cedric. He was surprised. He had improved his all-around game, although he doubted he

In only two years, Cedric (#31) became Cal State Fullerton's fourth-highest scorer.

ANDERSON ELEMENTARY SCHOOL

Cedric's college stats at Ventura Junior College (1986–88) and Cal State Fullerton (1988–90)

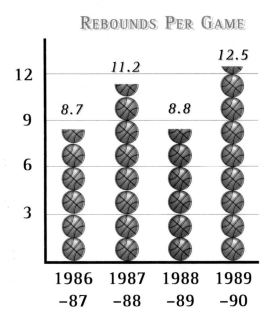

REBOUNDS PER GAME

1986 -87	1987 -88	1988 -89	1989 -90
8.7	11.2	8.8	12.5

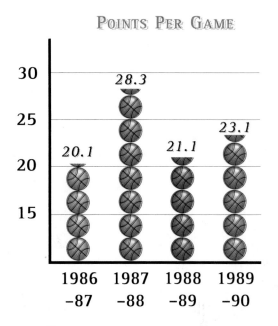

POINTS PER GAME

1986 -87	1987 -88	1988 -89	1989 -90
20.1	28.3	21.1	23.1

could make it in the NBA. In fact, Cedric never thought of himself as NBA material. "I thought I'd play two years of basketball, graduate, and get on with my life," Cedric recalls. "I didn't have any intention of playing in the NBA." But the scouts saw a young man with a knack for being in the right place at the right time. He had the talent to "finish" a play. Cedric possessed the kind of instincts that a coach cannot teach. If he could continue to develop his skills, he had a shot at a career in basketball.

The Story

In the second round of the 1990 NBA draft, the Phoenix Suns selected Cedric Ceballos, making him the 48th player chosen that day. The Suns already had a number of veterans who played Cedric's position, so nobody gave him much of a chance when training camp began. After all, what could a skinny 21-year-old offer a team that had won 54 games the year before?

But Cedric made the team by convincing the Suns that he had the hustle and desire to be a quality player off the bench. In his first two seasons in Phoenix, Cedric averaged about 11 minutes per game. He watched and learned, and as his body started to fill out, he discovered that he could score and rebound against some of the league's toughest players. He also began to understand that he could help the team even when he was not scoring.

NBA fans got their first real look at Cedric prior to the 1992 All-Star Game. He won the Slam Dunk contest in

Continues

unforgettable fashion. He called his winning dunk a "Hocus Pocus" dunk because he did it blindfolded! Later that year, he impressed everyone by averaging 13.5 points per game during the playoffs.

Cedric got his big chance the following season, when Phoenix dealt away two starters who had been playing in front of him. His court time doubled, and he responded by hitting 57.6 percent of his shots, which was the best mark in the NBA in 1992–93. More important, he provided the spark the Suns needed to advance to the NBA Finals. Cedric missed the Finals with a foot injury, and many fans believe that Phoenix would have beaten the Chicago Bulls had he been available.

In the 1992 Slam Dunk contest, Cedric scored a perfect 50 with his spectacular blindfolded dunk.

Cedric was traded from the Suns to the Lakers at the start of the 1994–95 season.

C edric spent one more year with the Phoenix Suns, establishing himself as one of the NBA's top young players. Though Charles Barkley and Kevin Johnson did most of the shooting, Cedric still managed to average 19.1 points per game.

A few weeks prior to the start of the 1994–95 season, Cedric was traded to the Los Angeles Lakers. He was back home, he was wearing the same purple and gold uniform his childhood heroes had worn, and he was the main attraction in the Laker offense. It was a dream come true. Cedric responded with his finest year as a pro, establishing himself as the team's leader and being selected to play in the All-Star team.

"I had to start doing things in a basket-ball game that made me an asset. I thought that if I wasn't scoring, I wasn't helping. Rebounding, good defense, pushing the ball—that's what a team needs."

Timeline

1990:
Joins the
NBA
Phoenix
Suns

1988: Enters
California State
University at
Fullerton

**1994: Traded to the
Los Angeles Lakers**

**1992: Wins the
NBA Slam Dunk
competition**

**1993:
Leads the
NBA with
a 57.6
field goal
percentage**

Game

Cedric plays tough one-on-one against Kendall Gill of the New Jersey Nets.

Action!

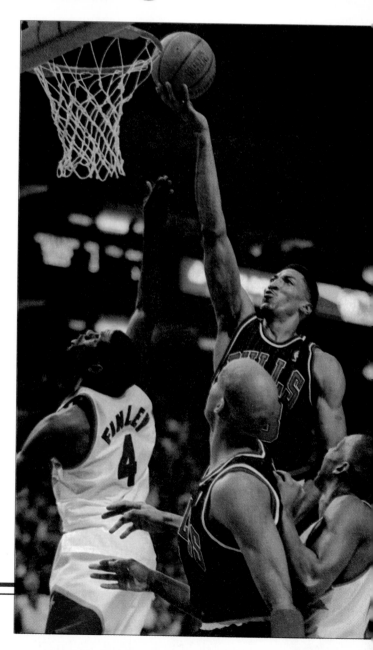

Coaches love Cedric because he does more than simply shoot and rebound. He hustles after loose balls, sets monster picks, and creates turnovers with his tremendous anticipation on defense.

Cedric and Scottie Pippen (right, with the ball) are considered the two finest rebounders among NBA small forwards.

ven in college Cedric did not know if he would make it in the NBA. "At the end of my senior year in college, pro scouts started coming to our games. I thought, 'If I'm drafted, I'll try it for a year.'"

hen Cedric scored a career-high 50 points in 1994, the first call he received was from former Phoenix teammate Charles Barkley (left). Sir Charles congratulated Cedric . . . and warned him he would never be able to score 50 against him!

edric is probably the only 20-point scorer in the league whose team runs no set plays for him. He gets all of his points by playing heads-up ball and creating his own shots.

Cedric's scoring bursts off the Phoenix bench earned him the nickname "Point-a-Minute Man."

The Suns did not believe Cedric could be a clutch player and often benched him in the fourth quarter of close games. What a mistake!

In college, Cedric's teammates called him "Ice" for his cool behavior on the court. His Laker teammates have revived the old nickname.

Cedric scoops up a loose ball from Eric Snow of the Seattle Supersonics.

Dealing

When Cedric Ceballos walked into Lakers training camp in September 1994, he was shocked. He had expected to join a proud team poised to bring the NBA title back to Los Angeles. Instead, Cedric found a collection of young players and uninspired veterans who did not understand that it took total commitment to win. Instead of screaming at his new teammates, he decided to set an example by arriving early, staying late, and playing all-out during practice. His teammates got the message, and the lowly regarded Lakers went all the way to the playoffs.

With It

edric felt pleased when his example had an effect on his teammates. "Suddenly, players are doing the same things I'm doing . . . people are getting on the same train."

HOW DOES

He Do It?

Ceballos can go head-to-head with any forward in the NBA. But he does his best work when he's running away from his man. When Cedric sees his defender take his eye off him, he sprints to an open spot on the floor and waits. If he sees a shot go up, he has a clear path to the basket. If a teammate drives, he angles toward the hoop for a possible pass. If he sees a loose ball, he dives to the floor and bats it to a fellow Laker. And if nothing happens, Cedric goes somewhere else and starts all over again!

"Movement is the key to my game."

The Grind

For an NBA player to give 100 percent mentally every night of the season, he needs something else to focus on when he is off the court. Cedric Ceballos likes to lose himself in the world of music. He has appeared on a music video and has recorded a number of rap songs, including "Flow On."

"I like to write and record music. I have a studio in downtown L. A., and I once worked with Quincy Jones. But I'm still learning. I hope to continue producing and performing when my playing days are over."

Say What?

What do basketball people say about Cedric Ceballos?

"You can't teach the quickness and nose for the ball that Cedric has."

—Paul Westphal,
former Phoenix Suns coach

"Cedric's a positive person. He believes in going out, trying as hard as he can as long as he's out there on the floor, and picking up his teammates as well."

—Kurt Rambis, former teammate

"He's so quick and sneaky. You look at him and say, 'this guy's got no game.' Then you look at the stats and he's killed you!"

—*Bill Walton, Hall of Fame center*

"If we'd had Cedric for the '93 Finals, we would have won the world championship."

—*Charles Barkley, former teammate*

"He has such a unique ability to get open. He's a very difficult guy to set a game plan against."

—*Del Harris, Los Angeles Lakers coach*

"Cedric is even better than I had thought. We knew he was good—that's why we wanted him so badly. But we'd only seen him in doses."

—*Magic Johnson, teammate*

Career

Highlights

edric's career mark of 22.1 points-per-game at Cal State Fullerton is still the top scoring average in school history.

edric led the NBA with a 57.6 shooting percentage in 1992–93. The next year he placed seventh with a 53.5 percent mark.

When Cedric made the 1994 All-Star team, he became the first Laker to do so since Magic Johnson and James Worthy played in the 1992 contest.

Cedric was named the NBA's Player of the Month in December 1994. He averaged 27.8 points and 9.0 rebounds per game during that stretch.

In his final season with the Suns, Cedric turned in a pair of 40-point games during the same week.

Cedric scored a career-high 50 points against the Timberwolves on December 20, 1994. Only six other players in Laker history have accomplished that feat.

Cedric's great performance in December 1994 earned him Player of the Month honors.

In 1994–95 Cedric led the Lakers in shooting percentage, despite a thumb injury that caused him to miss 22 games.

Cedric became the first player in Lakers history to convert a four-point play. In a 1995 game against the Portland Trailblazers, he was fouled while shooting a three-pointer, and then he made the free throw.

Cedric has such a high career shooting percentage because he goes to the basket so well.

Reaching

Cedric Ceballos loves working with kids. In 1995, when a labor dispute kept the players from going to training camp, he called a couple of his NBA pals and put together a free basketball camp for children near his home in California. Cedric is involved with the Boys and Girls Clubs of America, and he is also a big booster of the 65 Roses Foundation, an organization dedicated to seeking a cure for cystic fibrosis, a disease that affects mainly children.

Out

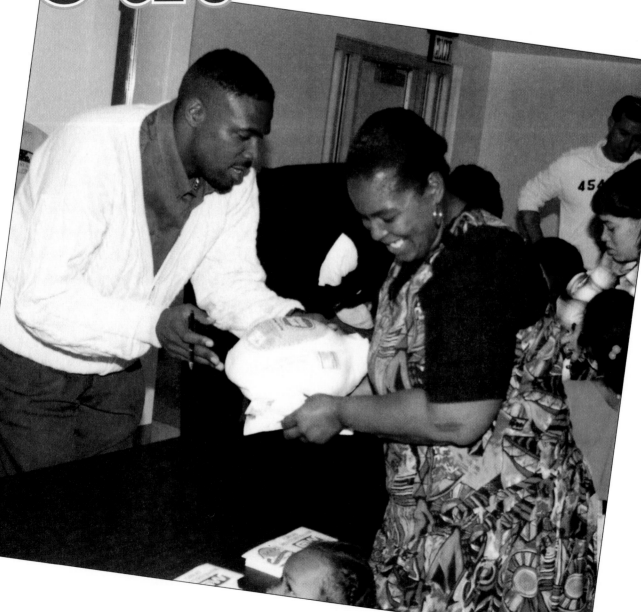

Numbers

Name: Cedric Z. Ceballos

Nickname: "Ice"

Born: August 2, 1969

Height: 6' 7"

Weight: 225 pounds

Uniform Number: 23

College: Cal State Fullerton

Cedric is one of only five Los Angeles Lakers in history to average over 20 points and 8 rebounds in the same season. The others are Kareem Abdul-Jabbar, Wilt Chamberlain, Elgin Baylor, and Magic Johnson—four of the greatest stars in NBA history!

Year	Team	Games	Rebounds	Rebounds Per Game	Points	Points Per Game
1990–91	Phoenix Suns	63	150	2.4	519	8.2
1991–92	Phoenix Suns	64	152	2.4	462	7.2
1992–93	Phoenix Suns	74	408	5.5	949	12.8
1993–94	Phoenix Suns	53	344	6.5	1,010	19.1
1994–95	Los Angeles Lakers	58	464	8.0	1,261	21.7
1995–96	Los Angeles Lakers	78	536	6.9	1,656	21.2
Totals		390	2,054	5.3	5,857	15.0

What If...

I never really thought about playing basketball for a living until right before I graduated from college. I was a communications major, which gave me skills that would have helped me in any career I chose. As it turned out, I ended up playing ball. But if I had not made it in the NBA, I would either be working with kids—like my brother, Chris—or doing something in the music business. I have a strong will, I'm a hard worker, and I always find a way to enjoy whatever I do. I think if you can approach life this way, and stay clear of bad influences, you have an excellent chance of being successful."

Glossary

ASSET advantage; resource

COMMUNICATIONS the study of how people relate to each other

CONVERT to change something into something different

REGARDED looked upon; considered to be

SCHOLARSHIP money given to a student to help pay for schooling

THRIVE to grow and be successful

TUITION money paid to attend a school or college

VETERAN one who has a lot of experience

DYSLEXIA a learning disability that affects a person's ability to read

MAJOR the main subject of courses one studies in college (a math *major* takes mostly math courses)

POISED in position; ready and waiting to complete a task

PREMIERE first in position, rank, or importance

Index

About The Author

Mark Stewart grew up in New York City in the 1960s and 1970s—when the Mets, Jets, and Knicks all had championship teams. As a child, Mark read everything about sports he could lay his hands on. Today, he is one of the busiest sportswriters around. Since 1990, he has written close to 500 sports stories for kids, including profiles on more than 200 athletes, past and present. A graduate of Duke University, Mark served as senior editor of *Racquet*, a national tennis magazine, and was managing editor of *Super News*, a sporting goods industry newspaper. He is the author of every Grolier All-Pro Biography.